Copyright © 2008 by Lomita Publishing. All rights reserved. This book, or any part thereof, may not be reproduced in any form without the written permission of the publisher.

Lomita Publishing
2940 Lomita Rd.
Santa Barbara, California 93105

Photographs copyrighted © by Chuck Place
chuckplace@placephotograpy.com

Text copyrighted © by Rachel S. Thurston
rsthurston@hotmail.com

Library of Congress
Cataloging-in-Publication Data
LCCN 2007906382 (soft cover)
LCCN 2007906380 (hard cover)

ISBN 978-0-9799008-0-8 (soft cover)
ISBN 978-0-9799008-1-5 (hard cover)

Book Design by Don French & Associates
and Scott F. Reid & Associates
Santa Barbara, California

Printed in Hong Kong
through Bolton Associates, Inc.
San Rafael, California

The Beautiful
SANTA YNEZ VALLEY

PHOTOGRAPHY BY CHUCK PLACE
TEXT BY RACHEL S. THURSTON

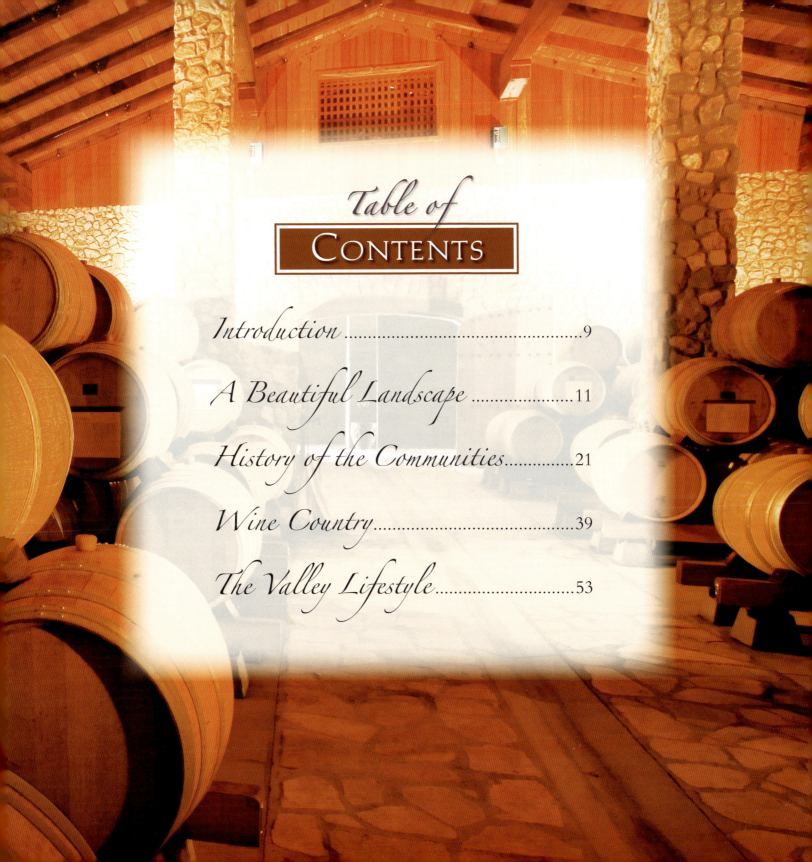

Table of Contents

Introduction 9

A Beautiful Landscape 11

History of the Communities 21

Wine Country 39

The Valley Lifestyle 53

INTRODUCTION

The sky is a brilliant blue, we've passed yet another row of grapevines and wild sage lightly scents the air. My friend and I are in search of a little market I remember coming upon years ago. We're somewhere between Los Olivos and the town of Santa Ynez, munching on strawberries we purchased earlier in the day at the farmer's market in Solvang. A woman with long blond hair is walking along the side of the road in a sundress, carrying a basket of raspberries, and we stop to ask for directions.

I describe the little market with the wooden sign to her and how it's at the end of a long gravel lane lined by a white picket fence. *Did I merely imagine it?* "Can't think of a market like that besides the one off Highway 154. But then, you never know around here," she adds with a bright smile.

We drive for the rest of the afternoon in circles beneath a warm summer sun, crossing our own tracks and pondering the illogic of country roads until we finally give up and stop at a small, shady cafe. We order a tasty dish of crispy shredded phyllo stuffed with warm goat cheese that's laid upon a bed of slightly sweet, pureed tomatoes. We dunk toasted crostada in the sauce and wash it down with glasses of chilled local Chardonnay. This is definitely a cut above your usual roadside cafe.

We never do find the market, but we are both pleasantly full and I feel rested in a way that I never do when I'm at home. As I finish off my glass of wine and feel the warmth of the early evening sun on my face, I decide that everything

is as it should be. It's just another great day in the valley.

Those of us living nearby have come here to escape the pressures of our daily lives and to nab a bit of sunshine when the coastal fog dampens our sun-loving sensibilities. For years, Santa Ynez Valley has been our secret spot. Blessed with warm days and cool nights, the Valley is a paradise where we've picnicked with our families among hillsides of blooming lupine and golden poppies, ventured over the pass for exotic dinners and locally produced wines, and persuaded our friends to bike long distances, plying them with promises of "rests" at as many wineries as our palates can handle.

With recent attention due to high-profile Hollywood films and a burgeoning wine industry that's bringing its own much-deserved international acclaim, the valley has become a destination for wine lovers, gourmands, and cultural adventurers of all ages. No matter how long one has lived or visited here, the valley continues to yield new surprises. Visiting Santa Ynez Valley is, in many ways, like entering the Old West, but with a twenty-first century twist: where cowboys talk on cell phones, Indians run casinos, and farmers raise ostriches. Its history is as rich as any in California. The Valley has managed to blend the flavors of Old World influences with contemporary sophistication.

From world-renowned wineries and horse ranches to outdoor theatre and festivals, the valley never has a shortage of things to do. In fact, with all of its draws, it's difficult for Santa Ynez Valley to stay out of the limelight. And so we share our beloved paradise with the rest of the world. *Welcome to Santa Ynez.*

A Beautiful LANDSCAPE

When you drive over the pass, a sensation may come over you, as if driving into California's past...the San Rafael Mountains spread out before you like an impressionist painting, their grasslands becoming a butterscotch color in the late afternoon sun. Below their steep slopes, ancient oak trees dot the hillsides with their magnificent, twisted forms.

It's difficult to believe that less than a hundred years ago, locals and merchants were traveling this same road by stagecoach. Chiseled into the rock and dirt of the mountainside, this precursor to Highway 154 was merely a route for travelers making their way from the train station in Los Olivos to downtown Santa Barbara. Rickety stagecoaches would make a long, dusty journey over a treacherous path frequented by bandits and grizzlies, both of which offered their own unique demise. That trip once took a full day.

Although the landscape of the valley has been shaped in years past by the hands of diligent farmers and builders, the most significant landmarks remain as they have been for the past millennium. Part of a deep sedimentary marine bed and a larger mountain range, the San Rafael and Santa Ynez Mountains were uplifted over a million years ago. Unique in their geology, they're one of only a handful of mountain ranges which stretch east to west, creating a parallel valley between. This orientation affects the local climate of the valley as well, making this the perfect region for growing wine grapes.

As you descend Highway 154 down into the valley, you will see the slender ribbon of the Santa Ynez River winding its way from the western edge of Lake Cachuma. Built half a century ago to trap the floodwaters of the river, Cachuma shimmers a deep azure, its colors shifting like moods in the mercurial light.

In the distance, the valley rolls forth in a patchwork of vineyards, beautiful in their symmetry. Fields of spearmint green alfalfa line the roads and small communities are nestled among vineyards and ranches, hidden until you're nearly upon them.

The mountainsides surrounding the valley are blanketed by *chaparral*, a native plant community perfectly adapted to this Mediterranean climate where sunshine is guaranteed and rain is not. While driving through the valley at sunset, it's not uncommon for a coyote to dash across your line of sight or for a doe and her fawn to amble across the country road in the dimming light.

The Seasons

With each season in the valley comes a subtle shift in light, color, and mood.

Spring brings an explosion of wildflowers on the rolling hills and slopes. Violet stalks of lupine thrust up through the grass beside bunches of bright California poppies, rich in their tangerine hues. Fields of silver-grey lavender bushes are beginning to bloom, swaying like sea anemones in tightly clumped fields.

By midsummer, the hills dry up as if burnt by fire and the grass has curled in on itself and turned the color of toffee. Raspberries and blackberries dangle like gems among thorns. Ripe peaches drip from their branches. The hills of chaparral seem to crackle in the heat. A red-tailed hawk lands on a nearby fence post, alert and hungry.

Fall heralds a crisp coolness in the air and pumpkin patches swell with their lantern-like fruit. Rows of corn rustle in the breeze while Canadian geese make their way south. The foliage of sycamore trees turns a dark lemon meringue and leaves flit off in the wind and feather their way back down to the ground. Apple and walnut trees are laden with their bounty.

Fall is also the time for harvesting the grapes. The vines are heavy with fruit, clumps of Syrah grapes with their deep purple black skins look as if they've been dusted with sugar. Translucent clusters of Chardonnay shimmer with morning dew, their sugar content high.

Winter is only slightly cooler than autumn, but the locals can feel it…in the chill, the short daylight hours, and the fact that they might have to actually wear a light jacket to dinner. This is the time when the valley gets most of its precious rainfall and, for a short time, the Santa Ynez River will become swollen and travel swiftly like it once did before the time of dams and unquenchable urban thirst.

During this wet season, the grass, oak trees, and shrubs soak up this precious gift, their leaves beginning to bud. The landscape is given lease on another year of life and wildflowers burst up from the dampened soil.

Above: Mule deer fawn in tall grass. Opposite: Lupine and blue oaks on Figueroa Mountain.

Nestled between two mountain ranges and fed by the Santa Ynez River, scenic Lake Cachuma is popular among large numbers of campers, fishermen, and wildlife-viewing enthusiasts.

Strong as an OAK

Once an essential food source to the Chumash and Indians throughout California, oak acorns were leached of their tannins and turned into mush, bread, and soup. Used on multiple levels throughout Native American cultures in California, the oak tree was the symbol of fertility, good luck, and has even been documented as being placed with burials as a food source in the afterlife.

By the early 1900s, as much as 90% of California's valley oak riparian forests had been destroyed to make way for farmland and grazing. Like many of the regions in Northern California, oaks in Santa Ynez Valley were destroyed to make way for agriculture. Of the nine native species of oak trees found throughout California, six occur in Santa Ynez Valley: the valley oak, blue and black oak, coast live oak, interior live oak, and canyon oak. Ironically, the sight of these centuries-old trees amidst rows of grapevines and cattle grasslands has become one of the most iconic images associated with the Valley.

History of the Communities

History of the Communities

For many, it's a challenge to understand the valley's layout with its circuitous roads and mysteriously placed towns…nothing seems easy to find and everything seems off the beaten track.

The more one explores the towns, however, the more they appear to be connected: collectively bound to the whims of history and fate. Each of the communities has had its share of the limelight, whether it was the arrival of the narrow-gauge train in nineteenth century Los Olivos or the Danish royal visits to Solvang in the twentieth century. If you look closely, the towns' histories are etched on their architectural style and their character.

In many ways, the Santa Ynez Valley is a tapestry of dashed dreams and surprising resurrection. The Valley has seen the fall of the indigenous peoples and their economic climb back, the passage of stagecoaches and trains, and the arrival of the automobile and highway. The old has mixed with the new and turned Santa Ynez into a melting pot of the ages…a little Frontier, a dose of Victorian, a dash of European, and a sprinkle of rural Americana. Throughout the infinite number of challenges the past several centuries have brought to the Valley, its people have continued to endure, adapt, and flourish.

The Chumash and the Mission Era

When the Spanish arrived on the coast of Southern California in the autumn of 1542, the Chumash Indian territory

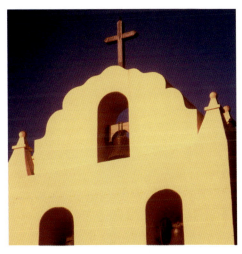

was the most densely populated region of California. An estimated eighteen thousand Chumash lived in villages spread out between modern-day Malibu and Paso Robles. At the time, the Santa Ynez Valley, like much of historic California, was covered in oak woodland and savannahs. Grizzly bears, mountain lions, and coyotes roamed the landscape and the Santa Ynez River was mightier and wider than it is today.

Known as the "Bead Money Makers," the Chumash were famed for their highly developed economy and their use of money carved from the Olivella seashell. They lived in well-organized villages, boasted a grasp of astronomy that rivaled the Europeans at the time, and were among only a few Native American groups on the West Coast of North America who were regular seafarers. Using only flint as a tool, the Chumash constructed long seaworthy plank canoes called *tomols* to travel along the coast and between the Channel Islands and the mainland.

The arrival of the Spanish during the sixteenth century was only the beginning of great change for this ancient culture. From the mid 1700s to the early 1800s, Franciscan priests sent by the Catholic Church undertook the establishment of a series of outposts, pueblos, and missions stretching nearly six hundred miles in length from San Diego up to Sonoma County. These outposts, positioned thirty miles apart, spanned a distance that could be covered in one long day on horseback.

In 1804, Father Estevan Tapis established Mission Santa Inés, located near present-day Solvang on a bluff overlooking a beautiful river. Taking its name after a fourth century Christian saint, Mission Santa Inés would officially become the nineteenth out of twenty-one missions, one of the last missions to be built during the Mission Era of California. Its name would eventually become anglicized to "Santa Ynez" and would become the namesake for not only the surrounding valley, but also for the river that it looked down upon as well as a neighboring frontier town.

BALLARD

Founded in 1881

Ironically, the first of the valley's communities is now the smallest and most overlooked by the majority of visitors. With quiet neighborhoods and just a few historic sites, Ballard is the epitome of a small town paradise. The roads feel like sleepy lanes as one rolls past picket fences and neatly kept porches where cottage-like homes are painted sea shell pink, turquoise, coffee, and canary yellow, their colors contrasted against crisp white trim.

Beneath the rustic calm of Ballard lies an unexpected love triangle. In the mid 1800s, a man by the name of Lewis settled on a ranch nearby called "El Alamo Pintado," meaning "painted cottonwood." Lewis was called away to Mexico on a business trip and asked his trusted friend, William Ballard, a superintendent of a rather extensive section of stage line stretching from Arizona to California, to watch his place. Several years later, caretaker Ballard became seriously ill and sent for his fiancé Cynthia. According to one romantic account of this story, Ballard's last wish before he died, was that his best friend Lewis return to the United States to marry Cynthia.

In memory of their good friend, the two were married and went on to found the town of Ballard in 1881. For years, Ballard enjoyed its position as the central hub for social activity and commerce in the valley as it had become a main stagecoach stop. As a testament to the town's legend, two streets in Ballard were named "Lewis" and "Cynthia."

SANTA YNEZ

Founded in 1882

Arguably the most western of all the communities in the valley, Santa Ynez was founded only a year after Ballard. Originally called "New Town," Santa Ynez was located along the stagecoach route between Santa Barbara and the North. During its heyday in the 1890s, the town boasted several saloons, a barbershop, mercantile store, blacksmith shops, ice cream parlor, Chinese quarter, and a Victorian-style hotel.

Today it doesn't take a stretch of the imagination to envision life here during the turn of the nineteenth century when horses were the chosen mode of transportation between ranches and town. Santa Ynez could easily be lifted from the pages of an old western, reminiscent of Texas hill country where cowboys and lawlessness ruled the land. Sitting down for breakfast over a plate of hot buttermilk biscuits with sausage gravy and a mug of black coffee, it's not uncommon to listen to waitresses greet the regulars in the morning as a small group of preteen boys strut by in their leather boots with cell phones in hand. Much of the action in the town of Santa Ynez happens near Maverick's, a popular historic saloon and bar in the valley, and up the road at the feed store where the

juiciest gossip in town is undoubtedly heard. Although it boasts countless top-notch wineries, galleries, and restaurants, Santa Ynez has at least one foot planted firmly in its historic roots.

LOS OLIVOS

Founded in 1887

In the late 1880s, the final tracks of the Pacific Coast Railroad arrived near an old stagecoach stop in Los Olivos. With the highly anticipated arrival of the train, passengers were able to travel by railway from the North and then transfer to a stagecoach for the journey over the mountains into Santa Barbara. During this early period, train conductors–probably bored spending too much time on a narrow gauge train through vast lengths of wilderness populated by grizzlies and mountain lions–nicknamed Los Alamos "Lost Almost" and Los Olivos as "Lost Altogether."

During the height of stagecoach and train travel, hotels, restaurants, stores, a school, and post office sprang up to meet the demands of the growing town. Mattei's Tavern, built in 1886 by Felix Mattei, served as a restaurant and resting place, and featured a barn where horses and stagecoaches were kept overnight. To this day, the tavern is a famous historic landmark and a restaurant representative of Los Olivos' frontier days.

Less than two decades after the arrival of the train, another technology signaled immutable change: the automobile. Highways were constructed throughout America to accommodate this revolutionary mode of travel. Los Olivos' residents assumed that the Coast Highway would pass through Los Olivos on its way to Santa Barbara. The State of California had other plans, and for reasons which were largely political, the highway ended up bypassing most of the valley and going through the Buell Ranch instead, site of the future town of Buellton.

Much of Los Olivos' history today is reflected in its architecture. While the town has become a renowned destination for epicureans, art collectors, and wine lovers, its great charm lies in what it has retained from its past: a unique blend of Western style storefronts scattered among Victorian style homes. Streets are lined with tasting rooms, upper class restaurants, a Western wear shop, market, art galleries, and an inn. In keeping with small town charm, one retailer has its own resident chickens that go by names like "Queenie," "Babs," and "Gertya."

CHUMASH

Reservation
Founded in 1901

The smallest of the valley's communities, by population, is inhabited by Native Americans who once numbered in the tens of thousands throughout the area. Today, there are some five thousand Americans proudly claiming Chumash heritage. Although the arrival of Europeans was initially a disaster for the Chumash—as it was for many Native Peoples—the Chumash have managed to adapt and to flourish again.

Today the Santa Ynez Band of Chumash Indians is the only federally recognized Chumash tribe in the United States. One of the newest developments in the valley has been the construction of the Chumash Casino Resort. The casino, which attracts thousands of people per day, has recently become a major player in the economic future of the area. In recent years, the Chumash Tribe has become one of the largest employers in the valley. A portion of the revenue gleaned from this business has allowed the tribe to put money into improved health care and educational opportunities for the Santa Ynez Chumash descendants. The tribe also continues to donate to organizations throughout the valley like the Santa Ynez High School, the County Fire Department, the local hospital, and various non-profit organizations.

SOLVANG

DANISH FOR "SUNNY FIELD"

Founded in 1910

Perhaps more surprising than finding a town inspired by the railroad or by a love triangle is stumbling upon a compact European-like village filled with Danish pastry shops, streets named after famous Vikings, and Scandinavian style architecture in the middle of a valley largely dominated by American Frontier themes. Although this European flair has been enhanced in some part to attract tourists, Solvang's cultural roots are undeniably authentic.

During the early 1900s, countless people were coming to the valley in search of farmland. In 1910, a group of Danish-American reverends and teachers sent by the Danish Lutheran Church in Michigan traveled to the area and purchased nine thousand acres for roughly $40 per acre. These proud Danes had aspirations of founding a colony that would include a Lutheran Church and a folk school where Danish-Americans could preserve their cultural heritage. Danish-Americans steadily flowed into the community, attracted to modestly-priced land and the allure of preserving their traditions.

In 1946, Solvang's unique cultural draw was featured in the national publication, *The Saturday Evening Post*, and the town's merchants, inspired by national attention, were

Opposite: Solvang is decked in Christmas lights. Above: Bread and pastries adorn a bakery window.

collectively mobilized to take on a more Scandinavian style of architecture. Since then, the town's businesses have been transformed into an architectural form characterized by tile and wood-shingled roofs, crisply painted trim, and thick lattice work. Some have remarked that Solvang, with its affinity for tradition and European aesthetics, is more Danish than Denmark itself.

To this day, Solvang's ties to its roots and motherland are strong. Eight percent of residents in Solvang claim Danish ancestry and visitors from around the world come to the town to celebrate their own Danish ancestry and to trace their family heritage.

Right: Traditionally-dressed dancer at Solvang's Danish Days Parade. Above: Beer steins, clogs, and tulips are available for purchase in Solvang.

Stagecoaches of the
OLD WEST

If you're wondering if stagecoaches are anything like the carriages depicted in old westerns, you're right. These vehicles were usually pulled by four horses and were vital to the development of the American West. Although the railroad arrived in the valley by 1887, it was too labor intensive to extend the railway up rugged and mountainous inclines like the Santa Ynez Mountains. Instead, stagecoaches were enlisted to make the last leg of the journey, often taking at least an extra half-day of travel.

For passengers traveling from the Santa Ynez Valley into Santa Barbara, they boarded a stagecoach in Los Olivos and made a treacherous and dusty ride over the San Marcos Pass, usually stopping for a hot meal and the changing and addition of new horses at the halfway point, the historic Cold Spring Tavern. This must have been an unforgettable adventure as stagecoaches were often preyed upon by bandits who hoped to rob coaches carrying payrolls and bank transfers. As if bandits and unexpected wildlife encounters weren't enough, the stagecoaches also had to deal with landslides and treacherous river crossings when the Santa Ynez River would become swollen with winter rains. Several horses perished during these ill-fated crossings.

BUELLTON

Founded in 1920

Known as a gateway city, the fastest growing community in the valley has, like many of the other towns, had its share of economic ups and downs.

In 1918, while Los Olivos was building itself up in anticipation of a highway that would never come, a bridge was constructed over the Santa Ynez River and consequently extended the Coast Highway through the Buell Ranch. This put the Buell Ranch property in a strategic location along one of the most important highways in California. As fortune would have it, the future site of Buellton was poised to prosper and make a name for itself in American history.

Because of its prime location along the Highway, Buellton was blessed with a growth boom: countless motels, service stations, and restaurants sprang up virtually overnight. During a time in America when families were taking to the road and discovering their country, Buellton was a model of development for a town built around the country's highway system. In 1949, the town was given the honor of being dubbed, "Service Town, U.S.A."

Unfortunately, so much traffic was passing through Buellton – imagine eight lanes of traffic moving through your hometown at high speeds – that it was creating countless fatal car crashes. Despite the protests of concerned business owners, the State Highway Department mandated that the 101 be rerouted out of downtown Buellton and be resituated in its present location. Andersen's Pea Soup, begun in 1924 with a sign that simply advertised "Eats," is the oldest continuously run business in the town and has dedicated a museum on its second floor to the town's golden years.

Although the arrival of the Coast Highway has brought more traffic to the area via Buellton, many of the Valley's winding roads evoke a more pastoral era.

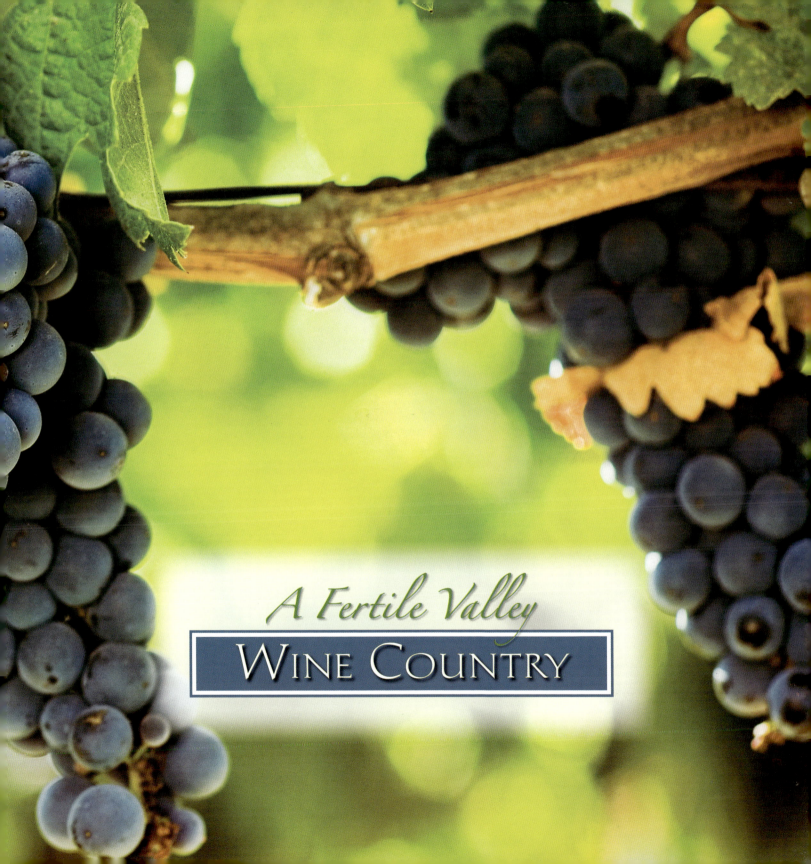

A Fertile Valley
WINE COUNTRY

A Fertile Valley
Wine Country

The frenetic guitar riff of the vintage surf song "Wipeout" cuts across the lawn as a barefoot woman and I collide in our effort to reach a barrel first. Everywhere around us, men, women, and youngsters are kicking off their shoes and jumping into one.

I run over to a barrel that reaches my chest and my friend and I hop in. The grapes squish between my toes like a cross between an expensive spa moisturizer and a haunted house experiment gone awry. It's icky and oozy and wonderful all at once.

People are bumping into each other with laughter. I ask the manager what they'll do with all of the now decimated grapes that sink beneath our weight.

"We'll use them of course," he winks at me with a devilish grin, which makes it difficult to discern whether he's joking or not. "This is a winery!"

All around the valley, wineries are celebrating their fall harvest in similar fashion, but with their own personal twist. Forty years ago, if you had told a local that grapes would one day be one of the most lucrative crops in Santa Barbara county or that an Academy Award nominated film would be made featuring Santa Ynez wine country, he probably would have laughed in your face. Although wine grapes have been grown in the county for over two centuries, Santa Ynez's late blooming wine industry was virtually nonexistent only a few decades ago. Since that time, Santa Ynez Valley has made a name for itself, not only in its production

of world class wines, but in the unique cultural experiences offered by each winery.

History of the Wine Grape

As in much of California, the first people to bring grapevines to the area were Franciscan missionaries. Historically, missions throughout California were encouraged to be self-sufficient and so, consequently, were required to grow their own food and make their own wine. As if by divine intervention, the Mediterranean climate of the region was quite similar to that of Spain's.

A Grape Idea Takes Root

In the 1960s two bold viticulturists, Uriel Nielson and Bill DeMattei, took a financial risk and planted acreage devoted entirely to wine grapes. After four years of planting and tending to a selection of varietals, including Cabernet Sauvignon, Chardonnay, and Sauvignon Blanc, the wine mavericks harvested their first grapes. Their venture paid off and news quickly spread of their success and the high quality of their grapes, which some boldly claimed, eclipsed that of Napa Valley.

Over the following years several other pioneering growers followed suit and began planting wine grapes, shipping their crops to Napa and other winemaking regions throughout the state. Eventually, a few of these first wine growers recognized that they had the ability to not just grow high quality grapes, but to produce esteemed wine as well. Among these early vintners was the

Firestone Family, who established the first estate winery in which the family lives on the premises where the wine is grown, produced, sold, and distributed.

In 1977 the Santa Ynez Valley Winery, established by Bettencourt-Davidge, won a gold medal at the Los Angeles County Fair for their Sauvignon Blanc and Semillon blend. The following year Firestone won a Double Gold Medal in London for their Chardonnay. The stakes were raised and the Santa Ynez Valley had officially caught the attention of wine lovers and vintners worldwide. A winemaking revolution had begun.

In the years since, countless awards have been bestowed upon wines produced throughout the Valley. The local wine industry now boasts nearly one hundred wineries and has grown to be the most lucrative of all industries in the county.

LOCATION! LOCATION! LOCATION!

Because of the unique east-west direction of Santa Ynez Valley, ocean breezes and coastal fog are swept inland, warming the region during the day and cooling it at night. Due to this geologic anomaly and the length of its corridor, the Valley provides a surprisingly wide range of soil types and temperatures.

Many visitors who enjoy wine tasting in Santa Ynez Valley rarely recognize that when they cross the 101 heading west from Buellton, they're entering a distinctly different winemaking region. The differences are vast enough between Santa Ynez Valley and the Santa Rita Hills that completely different varietals are grown within miles of each side of Highway 101.

With its wide range of soils and warmer average temperatures, Santa Ynez Valley has become known for specializing in high quality Bordeaux (Cabernet Sauvignon, Cabernet Franc, and Merlot), and Rhone (Syrah, Viognier, and Roussanne) wines. The slightly cooler and windier Santa Rita Hills region, which lies in between Buellton and Lompoc, has become well known for growing major Burgundy wines like Chardonnay and Pinot Noir as well as a few Italian and Rhone varietals.

Although each viticultural area has its specialties, there are an infinite number of microclimates within each region, based on soil, temperature, altitude, and proximity to the ocean. As you travel between the wineries, you will discover that neighboring wineries often grow completely different varietals, based on their vineyards' growing conditions.

Wineries with
FLAIR

While the valley has achieved widespread acclaim throughout the world for its wines, much of what makes this winemaking region special lies in the unique personalities and intimate sizes of its wineries, many of which are family owned. By sheer numbers, the county doesn't produce a large volume of wine, roughly a million cases per year. But what it lacks in overall production, it makes up for in quality and unerring panache.

Visitors aren't just connoisseurs in search of the most sublime Pinot Noir, they're families on weekend getaways or couples on their honeymoon. In fact, because of the personal draw that each of the wineries has developed, many businesses are focusing not just on their winemaking but on their appeal as a destination for weddings, corporate events, private parties, and concerts. Throughout the year several wineries host cooking classes, music concerts, and grape-stomping festivals and, in many ways, are becoming quite the hub for cultural activity throughout the valley.

On any given day, a couple will be exchanging vows surrounded by fragrant lavender and rosemary, a father and daughter will be learning to make a port wine reduction sauce and a young woman will try her hand at painting a watercolor label for a bottle of wine she has just purchased.

From intimate tasting rooms set out in small barns to buildings with cathedral ceilings and frontier-style chandeliers, Santa Ynez's wineries have no shortage of personality or flair. Thanks to several missionaries, hard-working farming families, viticulturists around the world, entrepreneurs, and a little good press, Santa Ynez, though a late bloomer, is quickly galvanizing its international reputation for its top wines and its endearing spirit.

From creating your own wine label or celebrating a winery on canvas to enjoying the company of a resident cat, the Valley's wineries offer an array of unique tasting experiences.

Wine Facts for Beginners
GRAPE TO GLASS

"Compromises are for relationships, not wine."

Sir Robert Scott Caywood

Part science, part art, and part instinct, winemaking is one of the oldest and most far-reaching traditions in the world, with its earliest evidence being traced back to an eight thousand year-old ceramic wine jar discovered in the former Soviet Republic of Georgia. Even Benjamin Franklin was so enraptured with the art of winemaking that he included his own recipe for fermenting wine grapes in his 1743 Farmer's Almanac. Whether you're an oenophile (that's "wine lover" for all you novices!) or not, it's difficult not to appreciate the amount of effort that goes into the production of wine from grape to glass. Here are a few facts about winemaking worldwide that may just help you appreciate your glass of Viognier that much more.

Winemaking and Grape Growing

- Approximately 500–600 grapes are needed to make one bottle of wine.
- It takes at least three years before most grapevines are capable of producing a harvest worthy of winemaking. When a vine reaches around 25–30 years of age, it produces fewer grapes but of a higher quality. In the United States, where quantity and keeping prices low is often valued above quality, many vineyards tear out these older vines and replant.
- One of the most expensive elements of winemaking is the oak barrel, which may range in price from $300–$850 and up. There are three main types of oak: American, Hungarian, and French, all of which lend their own unique flavors. Winemakers usually "retire" the barrels after several years of use.
- The average age of a French oak tree used to make barrels is one hundred and seventy years.
- Because of its alcohol content, no human pathogens can survive in wine.

Wine Consumption

- California accounts for 90% of America's total wine production.
- The United States ranks as the fourth highest producer of wine in the world.
- Americans drink an average of two gallons of wine per person annually.
- Chardonnay is the most popular wine in California and has been planted throughout most wine regions in the world. The Chardonnay grape is also one of the primary grapes used in the production of Champagne.

The Santa Ynez Valley Lifestyle

It's 10:45 p.m. and the dance floor at Maverick's is pleasantly packed. The wooden floors vibrate with the pulse of country music while men and women clad in cowboy boots and hats, jeans, and skirts spin past us in a giant circle. Above us are red, white, and blue neon-lit signs advertising cold American beers. Once again my feet get crushed beneath the weight of my partner's shoes.

He bites his lips apologetically. We're both doing our best to blend whatever swing dance moves we have and pass them off as country western moves. If we're in Santa Ynez on a Friday night, dang it, we're going to two-step! I look down at my scraped toes and we both wince. He gives me a look that asks how a country girl like me could possibly brave a two-stepping dance floor without the protection of cowboy boots or closed-toed shoes.

I get an idea that only a glass of wine and the brilliance of Friday night can bring on. "Hold on, I'll be right back."

I run outside to my car. If I can't have the right footwear then I'll just have to settle for the right hat wear. I search in back for my cowboy hat lined with turquoise beads and I head back to the saloon, slightly conscious of my mid-evening wardrobe change and wondering if I'll be judged by one of the cowboys outside for being an urban *poseur*.

To my great horror, the hefty bouncer puts his hands out. "You're going to have to stop right there," he says sternly.

He looks me up and down, taking careful note of my new head attire. Suddenly, he breaks into a grin of approval.

"Now we're talking," he says. His group of cowboy friends all motion me in.

It's difficult not to be pleasantly surprised by the characters you encounter in the Valley.

Horse Culture and Cattle Country

Late one hot morning in June, a waitress slides two plates of chili cheese omelets down in front of a friend and me. We sip on ice water to ward off the rising heat of the day.

On the main street, the Santa Ynez Day parade is slowly making its way up the street in front of us with the Elks Lodge members in the lead. A miniature horse pulls a cart with a woman dressed in an Old Frontier costume and a couple of compact, graceful horses trot by, their manes groomed like Mohawks.

"What kind of horse is that?" I ask our waitress.

She pivots towards the horses, squinting her eyes against the glare of the midday Santa Ynez sun. "I don't know," she says. "A mare?"

Whether you're a horse person or not, it's difficult not to appreciate how much of the Valley's history has been inextricably linked to horses. Santa Ynez Days is the quintessential way to experience the relationship that many valley residents have with cowboy culture.

Every summer the town turns out for the parade to feast on BBQ chicken,

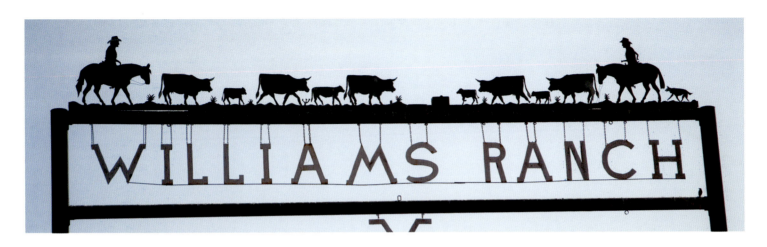

tri-tip, and strawberry shortcake and to watch festivities that only a small town with charm can attract. Vintage tractors chug along at sluggish speeds, the Santa Ynez High School Band plays classic marches, and several breeds of horses are shown off with their well-dressed riders in perfect form atop Western saddles.

Just up the street, the Santa Ynez Valley Historical Society has lovingly dedicated much of its museum to the horse culture of the valley. From small family-run farms to large breeding operations, the valley is a horse-lover's paradise. Nearly three dozen breeds of horses are found throughout the valley from the classic American Quarter Horse and American Paint to more exotic breeds like the long-living Icelandics and the graceful Lipizzaners.

The valley has also been home to many local celebrities, both equine and human. Three Kentucky Derby winners were raised here and Monty Roberts, author of the best-selling memoir, *The Man Who Listens to Horses*, has made Santa Ynez his family's home for the past several decades. The renowned horse trainer's ranch "Flag Is Up Farms" serves as a rehabilitation center for abused horses, as an equestrian academy, and as a venue for educating the public about his revolutionary violence-free methods of training horses.

Miniature Work
HORSES
PULL MORE THAN THEIR WEIGHT

Diminutive in size, miniature horses were imported from Europe during the late 1800s for use in the coal mines where their small stature and strength—they can pull up to ten times their weight—made them ideal workers. Historically, these miniature horses were also kept as pets by European royalty.

There are a wide range of activities in the valley, from flying gliders and bicycling through the vineyards to golf and fishing.

Eat Your Way Through
THE VALLEY

It's difficult to spend any time in the valley without thinking of food. Roadside stands offer fresh raspberries and blackberries that burst in your mouth like summer, swollen peaches beg to be made into pies, and wineries feature chocolate dipping sauces laced with undertones of raspberries and Merlot. So many tastes, so little time.

It's all rather daunting really.

On a quest early one afternoon, I duck into a restaurant in Solvang, curious what the Danish cuisine is all about. I retreat from the heat into the cool of a restaurant that has been recommended to me by a local Danish woman at the Elverhøj Museum. Upon her fervent urging, I order a *smørrebrød*, an open-faced Danish sandwich. It's the perfect light summer lunch....two thin slices of a dense Danish rye topped with shavings of cool roast beef and a creamy horseradish sauce garnished with radishes, beets, and sweet pickles.

In the mood for something sweet, I visit a Danish bakery across the street and ask a baker which pastries are most typical of the Scandinavian country. She points out a few, all of which are covered in sugar and variable in their shapes. The "Kringles," which resemble giant baked pretzels, are scrumptious looking but appear to be more than I can handle on a hot afternoon. I opt instead for a long, baguette-shaped "Danish Waffle" which consists of two layers of flaky pastry stuffed with fresh cream and a ribbon of raspberry jam. Just in case its caloric content might dip below three digits, the waffle is dusted with an extra helping of raw sugar. When I bite into it, the sugar and crust melt on my tongue like snowflakes.

Halfway through my Danish Waffle, I swear I'll never eat again.

Later that day, I meet up with a group of friends for dinner. We feast on sautéed squash blossoms filled with goat cheese and pine nuts and savor a bottle of peach-accented Chardonnay. A young couple beside our table is enjoying a flourless chocolate torte in a warm caramel sauce topped with vanilla bean ice cream and dusted with cinnamon. We vow to order four of them immediately.

Whatever your aim in the valley, eating is certain to be a part of the agenda. The weekly farmer's market in Solvang features locally grown, seasonal fruits, vegetables, and flowers and caters to

locals, restaurant owners, and visiting epicureans. As visitation increases to the wineries, their services are expanding to suit the tastes of more than just wine lovers. One winery has begun hosting cooking classes with guest chefs. Students learn to prepare dishes like giant pans of paella, featuring steaming saffron rice, succulent chicken, mussels, and lobster.

Whether you're into stick-to-your ribs faire or haute cuisine, the valley is undeniably the ultimate destination for food lovers. From enjoying juicy slabs of tri-tip hot off the grill to street side cafes where you nibble on smoked mozzarella rolled in paper-thin prosciutto, the valley's eateries never disappoint. Not a parade or festival exists in the valley without some measure of loving attentiveness paid towards the food.

Festivals and SEASONS

Inspired by a visit from Danish royalty nearly three-quarters of a century ago, Solvang has been hosting the ever-popular Danish Days during harvest time. Scandinavian-proud residents don traditional costumes and participate in folk dancing, music, and festivities throughout the town. Vendors break out giant pans to fry up the Viking-inspired *aebleskivers*, round pancake-like puffs drizzled with raspberry jam and dusted with powdered sugar.

Throughout the summer, families and couples converge on the Pacific Conservatory of the Performing Arts Theaterfest in Solvang, which features musical and theatrical productions in an outdoor amphitheatre. Hunker down beneath a warm blanket under a full moon and sip from hot chocolate as you enjoy a playful Shakespearean piece.

With fall comes the celebration of the grape harvest. Several wineries host their own individual harvest celebrations where you have an opportunity to grab a glass of Syrah, hike your skirt up, and sink your bare feet into tubs of freshly-picked grapes which crush between your toes.

Getting a head start for the holidays, Solvang hosts a series of events for "Winterfest," decorating the trees for yuletide with garlands of sparkling lights while shops throughout town offer homemade cookies and cider to strolling patrons.

In the spring the Santa Barbara County Vintners' Festival celebrates the new season and vintages with music, wine, scrumptious food, and special events held among the wineries.

The valley hosts year-round attractions as well. The renowned Elverhøj Museum, named "Elves on a Hill" after a nineteenth century Danish folk tale, is one of the only museums outside of its homeland dedicated entirely to Danish culture. The museum features vibrant recreations of centuries old Danish living spaces and gives lace-making demonstrations in the Old World tradition.

Left: Old truck loaded with Halloween pumpkins near Solvang. Right: Viking re-enactor at Danish Days Parade in Solvang. Opposite: Riders in the Old Santa Ynez Day Parade, crowds of wine tasters at the Vintners' Festival in Lompoc.

The CULTURAL

Throughout the Valley, the arts flourish. In addition to renowned art and antique galleries, newer galleries continue sprouting from the fertile cultural ground found here. The Wildling Art Museum occupies a historic home in Los Olivos and exhibits artwork and photography of America's majestic wilderness areas. The Santa Ynez Valley Museum also features the Parks-Janeway Carriage House, which showcases one of the most extensive collections of stagecoaches found in the West. In addition to its museums, the Santa Ynez Valley Historical Society also hosts the annual "Vaquero Show," which celebrates the California cowboy and highlights western memorabilia. The Santa Ynez Band of Chumash Indians holds an annual Powwow honoring Native American dancers and drummers from around the country, while many wineries sponsor jazz and classical music concerts year-round.

Left: Traditional dancer at the Chumash Inter-Tribal Powwow at Live Oak Campground. Opposite: Painter at the Artist's Quickdraw and Auction in Los Olivos, young Hispanic dancers in the Old Santa Ynez Day Parade, banners mark the location of Solvang's Theaterfest, reconstructed Chumash hut at La Purisima Mission State Historic Park near Lompoc.

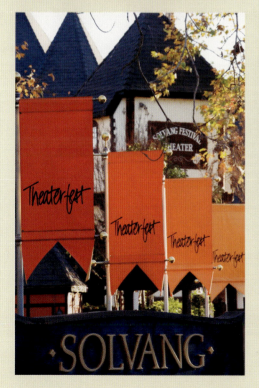

It is indeed ironic that being out of the way is now what draws people to Santa Ynez Valley. Urbanites flock here for rest and to escape the hectic strain of their jobs. For years, celebrities, artists, musicians, and politicians have been drawn to this region, as much for its cultural sophistication as for the anonymity that rural communities provide.

For as much as the valley has changed in the past few centuries, all the things that are right about it—the kindness of its people, its individuality, and its peacefulness—have stayed very much the same. It's because of this unique ability to adapt and yet remain unchanged through the ages that Santa Ynez continues to shine.

Acknowledgements

In my research on this book, I've turned to many resources, museums, and agencies that have provided me with wonderful insight. I would especially like to give thanks to the Santa Barbara County Vintners' Association, the County of Santa Barbara, the Santa Ynez Band of Chumash Indians, the Santa Ynez Valley Visitors Association, the Santa Ynez Valley Historical Society Museum and Parks-Janeway Carriage House, the Solvang Conference and Visitors Bureau, the Elverhøj Museum, Mission Santa Inés, Santa Barbara County Parks and Lake Cachuma, the Santa Barbara Museum of Natural History, the Santa Barbara Botanic Garden, *Inside The Santa Ynez Valley, Santa Ynez Valley Guest Magazine, The Santa Ynez Valley Journal, The Santa Ynez Valley News, Destination Wine Country*, the Los Olivos Rotary Club, the Buellton Historical Society and Andersen's Pea Soup, and Los Padres National Forest. My forgiveness if I've forgotten anyone!

Web Resources

Elverhøj Museum
www.elverhoj.org

Santa Ynez Band of Chumash Indians
www.santaynezchumash.org

Santa Barbara County Vintners' Association
www.sbcountywines.com

Santa Ynez Valley Visitors Association
www.syvva.com

The Buellton Historical Society
www.buelltonhistory.org

Santa Inés Mission
www.missionsantaines.org

County of Santa Barbara
www.countyofsb.org

Los Padres National Forest
www.fs.fed.us/r5/lospadres

Bibliography

Graham, Jr., Otis L., Sarah Harper Case, Victor W. Geraci, Susan Goldstein, Richard P. Ryba, Beverly J. Schwartzberg. *Aged In Oak: The Story of the Santa Barbara County Wine Industry*. Santa Ynez: Santa Barbara County Vintners' Association, 1998.

Head, W.S., *The California Chaparral: An Elfin Forest*. Happy Camp: Naturegraph Publishers, 1972.

Jackman, Jarrell C. *Santa Barbara: Historical Themes and Images*. Norfolk: The Donning Company, 1988.

Margerum, Hugh and David Powdrell. *A Field Guide to Common Plants of the Santa Barbara Foothills and Southern California*. Santa Barbara: Cismontane Publishing, 2005.

Olmstead, Cresencia and Dale. *Mission Santa Inés: The Hidden Gem*. Los Olivos: Cachuma Press, 1995.

Pavlik, Bruce M., Pamela C. Muick, Sharon Johnson, and Marjorie Popper. *Oaks of California*. Los Olivos: Cachuma Press, 1991.

Rife, Joanne. *Where the Light Turns Gold: The Story of the Santa Ynez Valley*. Fresno: Valley Publishers, 1977.